This record book belongs to: _____

Please call to return: _____

Thank you!

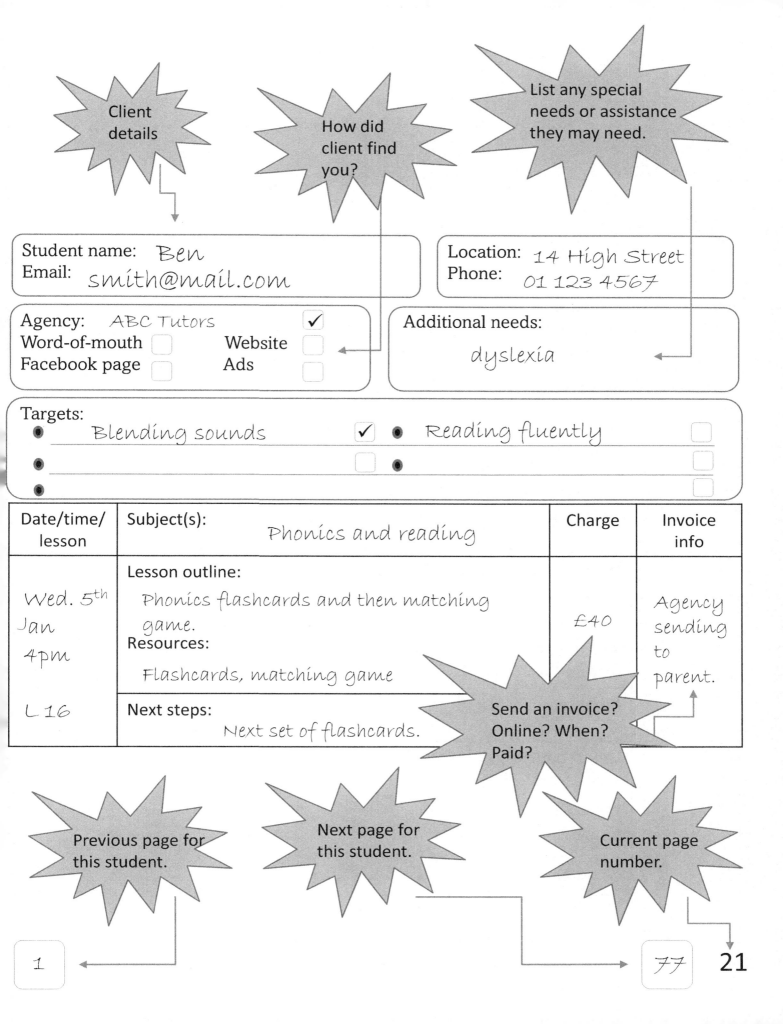

Student name:
Email:

Location:
Phone:

Agency:
Word-of-mouth ☐   Website ☐
Facebook page ☐   Ads ☐

Additional needs:

Targets:
- _____ ☐
- _____ ☐
- _____ ☐
- _____ ☐
- _____ ☐

Date/time/lesson	Subject(s):	Charge	Invoice info
	Lesson outline: Resources: Next steps:		
	Lesson outline: Resources: Next steps:		
	Lesson outline: Resources: Next steps:		

1

Date/time/ lesson	Subject(s):		Charge	Invoice info
	Lesson outline:			
	Resources:			
	Next steps:			
	Lesson outline:			
	Resources:			
	Next steps:			
	Lesson outline:			
	Resources:			
	Next steps:			
	Lesson outline:			
	Resources:			
	Next steps:			

Date/time/lesson	Subject(s):		Charge	Invoice info
	Lesson outline:			
	Resources:			
	Next steps:			
	Lesson outline:			
	Resources:			
	Next steps:			
	Lesson outline:			
	Resources:			
	Next steps:			
	Lesson outline:			
	Resources:			
	Next steps:			

Date/time/ lesson	Subject(s):	Charge	Invoice info
	Lesson outline: Resources: Next steps:		
	Lesson outline: Resources: Next steps:		
	Lesson outline: Resources: Next steps:		
	Lesson outline: Resources: Next steps:		

Student name:
Email:

Location:
Phone:

Agency: ☐
Word-of-mouth ☐ Website ☐
Facebook page ☐ Ads ☐

Additional needs:

Targets:
- _____ ☐
- _____ ☐
- _____ ☐
- _____ ☐
- _____ ☐

Date/time/ lesson	Subject(s):	Charge	Invoice info
	Lesson outline: Resources: Next steps:		
	Lesson outline: Resources: Next steps:		
	Lesson outline: Resources: Next steps:		

Date/time/ lesson	Subject(s):		Charge	Invoice info
	Lesson outline:			
	Resources:			
	Next steps:			
	Lesson outline:			
	Resources:			
	Next steps:			
	Lesson outline:			
	Resources:			
	Next steps:			
	Lesson outline:			
	Resources:			
	Next steps:			

Date/time/ lesson	Subject(s):		Charge	Invoice info
	Lesson outline:			
	Resources:			
	Next steps:			
	Lesson outline:			
	Resources:			
	Next steps:			
	Lesson outline:			
	Resources:			
	Next steps:			
	Lesson outline:			
	Resources:			
	Next steps:			

Date/time/ lesson	Subject(s):	Charge	Invoice info
	Lesson outline: Resources: Next steps:		
	Lesson outline: Resources: Next steps:		
	Lesson outline: Resources: Next steps:		
	Lesson outline: Resources: Next steps:		

Student name:
Email:

Location:
Phone:

Agency:
Word-of-mouth ☐   Website ☐
Facebook page ☐   Ads ☐

Additional needs:

Targets:
- ● _____   ● _____
- ● _____   ● _____
- ●

Date/time/ lesson	Subject(s):	Charge	Invoice info
	Lesson outline: Resources: Next steps:		
	Lesson outline: Resources: Next steps:		
	Lesson outline: Resources: Next steps:		

Date/time/lesson	Subject(s):	Charge	Invoice info
	Lesson outline: Resources: Next steps:		
	Lesson outline: Resources: Next steps:		
	Lesson outline: Resources: Next steps:		
	Lesson outline: Resources: Next steps:		

Date/time/ lesson	Subject(s):	Charge	Invoice info
	Lesson outline: Resources: Next steps:		
	Lesson outline: Resources: Next steps:		
	Lesson outline: Resources: Next steps:		
	Lesson outline: Resources: Next steps:		

Date/time/lesson	Subject(s):		Charge	Invoice info
	Lesson outline:			
	Resources:			
	Next steps:			
	Lesson outline:			
	Resources:			
	Next steps:			
	Lesson outline:			
	Resources:			
	Next steps:			
	Lesson outline:			
	Resources:			
	Next steps:			

Student name:
Email:

Location:
Phone:

Agency:
Word-of-mouth ☐   Website ☐
Facebook page ☐   Ads ☐

Additional needs:

Targets:
- _____ ☐
- _____ ☐
- _____ ☐
- _____ ☐
-

Date/time/ lesson	Subject(s):	Charge	Invoice info
	Lesson outline: Resources: Next steps:		
	Lesson outline: Resources: Next steps:		
	Lesson outline: Resources: Next steps:		

Date/time/ lesson	Subject(s):		Charge	Invoice info
	Lesson outline:			
	Resources:			
	Next steps:			
	Lesson outline:			
	Resources:			
	Next steps:			
	Lesson outline:			
	Resources:			
	Next steps:			
	Lesson outline:			
	Resources:			
	Next steps:			

Date/time/lesson	Subject(s):	Charge	Invoice info
	Lesson outline: Resources: Next steps:		
	Lesson outline: Resources: Next steps:		
	Lesson outline: Resources: Next steps:		
	Lesson outline: Resources: Next steps:		

Date/time/lesson	Subject(s):	Charge	Invoice info
	Lesson outline: Resources: Next steps:		
	Lesson outline: Resources: Next steps:		
	Lesson outline: Resources: Next steps:		
	Lesson outline: Resources: Next steps:		

Student name:
Email:

Location:
Phone:

Agency:
Word-of-mouth ☐ Website ☐
Facebook page ☐ Ads ☐

Additional needs:

Targets:
- ☐
- ☐
- ☐
- ☐
- ☐

Date/time/ lesson	Subject(s):	Charge	Invoice info
	Lesson outline: Resources: Next steps:		
	Lesson outline: Resources: Next steps:		
	Lesson outline: Resources: Next steps:		

17

Date/time/ lesson	Subject(s):		Charge	Invoice info
	Lesson outline:			
	Resources:			
	Next steps:			
	Lesson outline:			
	Resources:			
	Next steps:			
	Lesson outline:			
	Resources:			
	Next steps:			
	Lesson outline:			
	Resources:			
	Next steps:			

Date/time/lesson	Subject(s):	Charge	Invoice info
	Lesson outline: Resources: Next steps:		
	Lesson outline: Resources: Next steps:		
	Lesson outline: Resources: Next steps:		
	Lesson outline: Resources: Next steps:		

Date/time/ lesson	Subject(s):		Charge	Invoice info
	Lesson outline:			
	Resources:			
	Next steps:			
	Lesson outline:			
	Resources:			
	Next steps:			
	Lesson outline:			
	Resources:			
	Next steps:			
	Lesson outline:			
	Resources:			
	Next steps:			

Student name:
Email:

Location:
Phone:

Agency:
Word-of-mouth ☐   Website ☐
Facebook page ☐   Ads ☐

Additional needs:

Targets:
- _____ ☐   • _____ ☐
- _____ ☐   • _____ ☐
- _____   ☐

Date/time/ lesson	Subject(s):	Charge	Invoice info
	Lesson outline: Resources: Next steps:		
	Lesson outline: Resources: Next steps:		
	Lesson outline: Resources: Next steps:		

Date/time/ lesson	Subject(s):		Charge	Invoice info
	Lesson outline:			
	Resources:			
	Next steps:			
	Lesson outline:			
	Resources:			
	Next steps:			
	Lesson outline:			
	Resources:			
	Next steps:			
	Lesson outline:			
	Resources:			
	Next steps:			

Date/time/ lesson	Subject(s):	Charge	Invoice info
	Lesson outline: Resources: Next steps:		
	Lesson outline: Resources: Next steps:		
	Lesson outline: Resources: Next steps:		
	Lesson outline: Resources: Next steps:		

Date/time/lesson	Subject(s):			Charge	Invoice info
	Lesson outline:				
	Resources:				
	Next steps:				
	Lesson outline:				
	Resources:				
	Next steps:				
	Lesson outline:				
	Resources:				
	Next steps:				
	Lesson outline:				
	Resources:				
	Next steps:				

Student name:
Email:

Location:
Phone:

Agency:
Word-of-mouth ☐   Website ☐
Facebook page ☐   Ads ☐

Additional needs:

Targets:
- _____ ☐   • _____ ☐
- _____ ☐   • _____ ☐
- ☐

Date/time/ lesson	Subject(s):	Charge	Invoice info
	Lesson outline: Resources: Next steps:		
	Lesson outline: Resources: Next steps:		
	Lesson outline: Resources: Next steps:		

Date/time/ lesson	Subject(s):	Charge	Invoice info
	Lesson outline: Resources: Next steps:		
	Lesson outline: Resources: Next steps:		
	Lesson outline: Resources: Next steps:		
	Lesson outline: Resources: Next steps:		

Date/time/lesson	Subject(s):	Charge	Invoice info
	Lesson outline: Resources:		
	Next steps:		
	Lesson outline: Resources:		
	Next steps:		
	Lesson outline: Resources:		
	Next steps:		
	Lesson outline: Resources:		
	Next steps:		

Date/time/ lesson	Subject(s):	Charge	Invoice info
	Lesson outline: Resources: Next steps:		
	Lesson outline: Resources: Next steps:		
	Lesson outline: Resources: Next steps:		
	Lesson outline: Resources: Next steps:		

Student name:
Email:

Location:
Phone:

Agency:
Word-of-mouth ☐   Website ☐
Facebook page ☐   Ads ☐

Additional needs:

Targets:
- _____ ☐
- _____ ☐
- _____ ☐
- _____ ☐
-

Date/time/ lesson	Subject(s):	Charge	Invoice info
	Lesson outline: Resources: Next steps:		
	Lesson outline: Resources: Next steps:		
	Lesson outline: Resources: Next steps:		

Date/time/ lesson	Subject(s):	Charge	Invoice info
	Lesson outline: Resources: Next steps:		
	Lesson outline: Resources: Next steps:		
	Lesson outline: Resources: Next steps:		
	Lesson outline: Resources: Next steps:		

Date/time/lesson	Subject(s):		Charge	Invoice info
	Lesson outline:			
	Resources:			
	Next steps:			
	Lesson outline:			
	Resources:			
	Next steps:			
	Lesson outline:			
	Resources:			
	Next steps:			
	Lesson outline:			
	Resources:			
	Next steps:			

Date/time/ lesson	Subject(s):		Charge	Invoice info
	Lesson outline:			
	Resources:			
	Next steps:			
	Lesson outline:			
	Resources:			
	Next steps:			
	Lesson outline:			
	Resources:			
	Next steps:			
	Lesson outline:			
	Resources:			
	Next steps:			

Student name:
Email:

Location:
Phone:

Agency:
Word-of-mouth ☐   Website ☐
Facebook page ☐   Ads ☐

Additional needs:

Targets:
- _____ ☐   • _____ ☐
- _____ ☐   • _____ ☐
- _____   ☐

Date/time/ lesson	Subject(s):	Charge	Invoice info
	Lesson outline: Resources: Next steps:		
	Lesson outline: Resources: Next steps:		
	Lesson outline: Resources: Next steps:		

33

Date/time/ lesson	Subject(s):		Charge	Invoice info
	Lesson outline:			
	Resources:			
	Next steps:			
	Lesson outline:			
	Resources:			
	Next steps:			
	Lesson outline:			
	Resources:			
	Next steps:			
	Lesson outline:			
	Resources:			
	Next steps:			

Date/time/ lesson	Subject(s):		Charge	Invoice info
	Lesson outline:			
	Resources:			
	Next steps:			
	Lesson outline:			
	Resources:			
	Next steps:			
	Lesson outline:			
	Resources:			
	Next steps:			
	Lesson outline:			
	Resources:			
	Next steps:			

Date/time/ lesson	Subject(s):	Charge	Invoice info
	Lesson outline: Resources: Next steps:		
	Lesson outline: Resources: Next steps:		
	Lesson outline: Resources: Next steps:		
	Lesson outline: Resources: Next steps:		

Student name:
Email:

Location:
Phone:

Agency:
Word-of-mouth ☐   Website ☐
Facebook page ☐   Ads ☐

Additional needs:

Targets:
- _____ ☐
- _____ ☐
- _____ ☐
- _____ ☐
- _____ ☐

Date/time/lesson	Subject(s):	Charge	Invoice info
	Lesson outline: Resources: Next steps:		
	Lesson outline: Resources: Next steps:		
	Lesson outline: Resources: Next steps:		

Date/time/ lesson	Subject(s):	Charge	Invoice info
	Lesson outline: Resources: Next steps:		
	Lesson outline: Resources: Next steps:		
	Lesson outline: Resources: Next steps:		
	Lesson outline: Resources: Next steps:		

Date/time/lesson	Subject(s):		Charge	Invoice info
	Lesson outline:			
	Resources:			
	Next steps:			
	Lesson outline:			
	Resources:			
	Next steps:			
	Lesson outline:			
	Resources:			
	Next steps:			
	Lesson outline:			
	Resources:			
	Next steps:			

Date/time/ lesson	Subject(s):	Charge	Invoice info
	Lesson outline: Resources: Next steps:		
	Lesson outline: Resources: Next steps:		
	Lesson outline: Resources: Next steps:		
	Lesson outline: Resources: Next steps:		

Student name:
Email:

Location:
Phone:

Agency:
Word-of-mouth ☐   Website ☐
Facebook page ☐   Ads ☐

Additional needs:

Targets:
- _____ ☐
- _____ ☐
- _____ ☐
- _____ ☐
- _____ ☐

Date/time/ lesson	Subject(s):	Charge	Invoice info
	Lesson outline: Resources: Next steps:		
	Lesson outline: Resources: Next steps:		
	Lesson outline: Resources: Next steps:		

Date/time/ lesson	Subject(s):		Charge	Invoice info
	Lesson outline:			
	Resources:			
	Next steps:			
	Lesson outline:			
	Resources:			
	Next steps:			
	Lesson outline:			
	Resources:			
	Next steps:			
	Lesson outline:			
	Resources:			
	Next steps:			

Date/time/ lesson	Subject(s):		Charge	Invoice info
	Lesson outline:			
	Resources:			
	Next steps:			
	Lesson outline:			
	Resources:			
	Next steps:			
	Lesson outline:			
	Resources:			
	Next steps:			
	Lesson outline:			
	Resources:			
	Next steps:			

Date/time/lesson	Subject(s):		Charge	Invoice info
	Lesson outline:			
	Resources:			
	Next steps:			
	Lesson outline:			
	Resources:			
	Next steps:			
	Lesson outline:			
	Resources:			
	Next steps:			
	Lesson outline:			
	Resources:			
	Next steps:			

Student name:
Email:

Location:
Phone:

Agency:
Word-of-mouth ☐   Website ☐
Facebook page ☐   Ads ☐

Additional needs:

Targets:
- _____ ☐
- _____ ☐
- _____ ☐
- _____ ☐
- _____ ☐

Date/time/ lesson	Subject(s):	Charge	Invoice info
	Lesson outline: Resources: Next steps:		
	Lesson outline: Resources: Next steps:		
	Lesson outline: Resources: Next steps:		

Date/time/ lesson	Subject(s):		Charge	Invoice info
	Lesson outline: Resources:			
	Next steps:			
	Lesson outline: Resources:			
	Next steps:			
	Lesson outline: Resources:			
	Next steps:			
	Lesson outline: Resources:			
	Next steps:			

Date/time/ lesson	Subject(s):	Charge	Invoice info
	Lesson outline: Resources:		
	Next steps:		
	Lesson outline: Resources:		
	Next steps:		
	Lesson outline: Resources:		
	Next steps:		
	Lesson outline: Resources:		
	Next steps:		

Date/time/lesson	Subject(s):		Charge	Invoice info
	Lesson outline:			
	Resources:			
	Next steps:			
	Lesson outline:			
	Resources:			
	Next steps:			
	Lesson outline:			
	Resources:			
	Next steps:			
	Lesson outline:			
	Resources:			
	Next steps:			

| Student name: | | Location: |
| Email: | | Phone: |

Agency:
Word-of-mouth ☐   Website ☐
Facebook page ☐   Ads ☐

Additional needs:

Targets:
- _____ ☐
- _____ ☐
- _____ ☐
- _____ ☐
- _____ ☐

Date/time/ lesson	Subject(s):	Charge	Invoice info
	Lesson outline: Resources: Next steps:		
	Lesson outline: Resources: Next steps:		
	Lesson outline: Resources: Next steps:		

Date/time/ lesson	Subject(s):	Charge	Invoice info
	Lesson outline: Resources: Next steps:		
	Lesson outline: Resources: Next steps:		
	Lesson outline: Resources: Next steps:		
	Lesson outline: Resources: Next steps:		

Date/time/lesson	Subject(s):	Charge	Invoice info
	Lesson outline: Resources: Next steps:		
	Lesson outline: Resources: Next steps:		
	Lesson outline: Resources: Next steps:		
	Lesson outline: Resources: Next steps:		

Date/time/lesson	Subject(s):		Charge	Invoice info
	Lesson outline: Resources:			
	Next steps:			
	Lesson outline: Resources:			
	Next steps:			
	Lesson outline: Resources:			
	Next steps:			
	Lesson outline: Resources:			
	Next steps:			

Student name:
Email:

Location:
Phone:

Agency:
Word-of-mouth ☐   Website ☐
Facebook page ☐   Ads ☐

Additional needs:

Targets:
- _____ ☐
- _____ ☐
- _____ ☐
- _____ ☐
- ☐

Date/time/ lesson	Subject(s):	Charge	Invoice info
	Lesson outline: Resources: Next steps:		
	Lesson outline: Resources: Next steps:		
	Lesson outline: Resources: Next steps:		

Date/time/ lesson	Subject(s):		Charge	Invoice info
	Lesson outline:			
	Resources:			
	Next steps:			
	Lesson outline:			
	Resources:			
	Next steps:			
	Lesson outline:			
	Resources:			
	Next steps:			
	Lesson outline:			
	Resources:			
	Next steps:			

Date/time/ lesson	Subject(s):	Charge	Invoice info
	Lesson outline: Resources: Next steps:		
	Lesson outline: Resources: Next steps:		
	Lesson outline: Resources: Next steps:		
	Lesson outline: Resources: Next steps:		

Date/time/ lesson	Subject(s):	Charge	Invoice info
	Lesson outline: Resources: Next steps:		
	Lesson outline: Resources: Next steps:		
	Lesson outline: Resources: Next steps:		
	Lesson outline: Resources: Next steps:		

Student name:
Email:

Location:
Phone:

Agency:
Word-of-mouth ☐ Website ☐
Facebook page ☐ Ads ☐

Additional needs:

Targets:
- ☐
- ☐
- ☐
- ☐
- ☐

Date/time/ lesson	Subject(s):	Charge	Invoice info
	Lesson outline: Resources: Next steps:		
	Lesson outline: Resources: Next steps:		
	Lesson outline: Resources: Next steps:		

Date/time/ lesson	Subject(s):		Charge	Invoice info
	Lesson outline:			
	Resources:			
	Next steps:			
	Lesson outline:			
	Resources:			
	Next steps:			
	Lesson outline:			
	Resources:			
	Next steps:			
	Lesson outline:			
	Resources:			
	Next steps:			

Date/time/lesson	Subject(s):	Charge	Invoice info
	Lesson outline: Resources:		
	Next steps:		
	Lesson outline: Resources:		
	Next steps:		
	Lesson outline: Resources:		
	Next steps:		
	Lesson outline: Resources:		
	Next steps:		

Date/time/lesson	Subject(s):		Charge	Invoice info
	Lesson outline:			
	Resources:			
	Next steps:			
	Lesson outline:			
	Resources:			
	Next steps:			
	Lesson outline:			
	Resources:			
	Next steps:			
	Lesson outline:			
	Resources:			
	Next steps:			

| Student name: | Location: |
| Email: | Phone: |

Agency:
- Word-of-mouth ☐
- Website ☐
- Facebook page ☐
- Ads ☐

Additional needs:

Targets:
- ☐
- ☐
- ☐
- ☐
- ☐

Date/time/lesson	Subject(s):	Charge	Invoice info
	Lesson outline: Resources: Next steps:		
	Lesson outline: Resources: Next steps:		
	Lesson outline: Resources: Next steps:		

61

Date/time/lesson	Subject(s):	Charge	Invoice info
	Lesson outline: Resources: Next steps:		
	Lesson outline: Resources: Next steps:		
	Lesson outline: Resources: Next steps:		
	Lesson outline: Resources: Next steps:		

Date/time/lesson	Subject(s):	Charge	Invoice info
	Lesson outline: Resources: Next steps:		
	Lesson outline: Resources: Next steps:		
	Lesson outline: Resources: Next steps:		
	Lesson outline: Resources: Next steps:		

Date/time/lesson	Subject(s):	Charge	Invoice info
	Lesson outline: Resources: Next steps:		
	Lesson outline: Resources: Next steps:		
	Lesson outline: Resources: Next steps:		
	Lesson outline: Resources: Next steps:		

Student name:　　　　　　　　　　　　　　　Location:
Email:　　　　　　　　　　　　　　　　　　　Phone:

Agency:　　　　　　　　　　　　　　　　　　Additional needs:
Word-of-mouth ☐　　Website ☐
Facebook page ☐　　Ads ☐

Targets:
- _____ ☐　● _____ ☐
- _____ ☐　● _____ ☐
- _____　　　　　　　　　　　　　　☐

Date/time/ lesson	Subject(s):	Charge	Invoice info
	Lesson outline: Resources: Next steps:		
	Lesson outline: Resources: Next steps:		
	Lesson outline: Resources: Next steps:		

Date/time/lesson	Subject(s):		Charge	Invoice info
	Lesson outline:			
	Resources:			
	Next steps:			
	Lesson outline:			
	Resources:			
	Next steps:			
	Lesson outline:			
	Resources:			
	Next steps:			
	Lesson outline:			
	Resources:			
	Next steps:			

Date/time/lesson	Subject(s):		Charge	Invoice info
	Lesson outline:			
	Resources:			
	Next steps:			
	Lesson outline:			
	Resources:			
	Next steps:			
	Lesson outline:			
	Resources:			
	Next steps:			
	Lesson outline:			
	Resources:			
	Next steps:			

Date/time/ lesson	Subject(s):		Charge	Invoice info
	Lesson outline:			
	Resources:			
	Next steps:			
	Lesson outline:			
	Resources:			
	Next steps:			
	Lesson outline:			
	Resources:			
	Next steps:			
	Lesson outline:			
	Resources:			
	Next steps:			

Student name: Email:		Location: Phone:	
Agency: Word-of-mouth ☐ Website ☐ Facebook page ☐ Ads ☐		Additional needs:	

Targets:
- ☐ _____
- ☐ _____
- ☐ _____
- ☐ _____
- ☐ _____

Date/time/ lesson	Subject(s):	Charge	Invoice info
	Lesson outline: Resources:		
	Next steps:		
	Lesson outline: Resources:		
	Next steps:		
	Lesson outline: Resources:		
	Next steps:		

Date/time/lesson	Subject(s):		Charge	Invoice info
	Lesson outline:			
	Resources:			
	Next steps:			
	Lesson outline:			
	Resources:			
	Next steps:			
	Lesson outline:			
	Resources:			
	Next steps:			
	Lesson outline:			
	Resources:			
	Next steps:			

Date/time/lesson	Subject(s):	Charge	Invoice info
	Lesson outline: Resources: Next steps:		
	Lesson outline: Resources: Next steps:		
	Lesson outline: Resources: Next steps:		
	Lesson outline: Resources: Next steps:		

Date/time/lesson	Subject(s):		Charge	Invoice info
	Lesson outline:			
	Resources:			
	Next steps:			
	Lesson outline:			
	Resources:			
	Next steps:			
	Lesson outline:			
	Resources:			
	Next steps:			
	Lesson outline:			
	Resources:			
	Next steps:			

Student name:
Email:

Location:
Phone:

Agency:
Word-of-mouth ☐   Website ☐
Facebook page ☐   Ads ☐

Additional needs:

Targets:
- _____ ☐
- _____ ☐
- _____ ☐
- _____ ☐
- _____ ☐

Date/time/ lesson	Subject(s):	Charge	Invoice info
	Lesson outline: Resources: Next steps:		
	Lesson outline: Resources: Next steps:		
	Lesson outline: Resources: Next steps:		

Date/time/lesson	Subject(s):		Charge	Invoice info
	Lesson outline:			
	Resources:			
	Next steps:			
	Lesson outline:			
	Resources:			
	Next steps:			
	Lesson outline:			
	Resources:			
	Next steps:			
	Lesson outline:			
	Resources:			
	Next steps:			

Date/time/lesson	Subject(s):	Charge	Invoice info
	Lesson outline: Resources: Next steps:		
	Lesson outline: Resources: Next steps:		
	Lesson outline: Resources: Next steps:		
	Lesson outline: Resources: Next steps:		

Date/time/lesson	Subject(s):	Charge	Invoice info
	Lesson outline: Resources: Next steps:		
	Lesson outline: Resources: Next steps:		
	Lesson outline: Resources: Next steps:		
	Lesson outline: Resources: Next steps:		

Student name:
Email:

Location:
Phone:

Agency:
Word-of-mouth ☐   Website ☐
Facebook page ☐   Ads ☐

Additional needs:

Targets:
- _____ ☐   • _____ ☐
- _____ ☐   • _____ ☐
- _____   ☐

Date/time/lesson	Subject(s):	Charge	Invoice info
	Lesson outline: Resources: Next steps:		
	Lesson outline: Resources: Next steps:		
	Lesson outline: Resources: Next steps:		

Date/time/ lesson	Subject(s):	Charge	Invoice info
	Lesson outline: Resources: Next steps:		
	Lesson outline: Resources: Next steps:		
	Lesson outline: Resources: Next steps:		
	Lesson outline: Resources: Next steps:		

Date/time/lesson	Subject(s):	Charge	Invoice info
	Lesson outline: Resources: Next steps:		
	Lesson outline: Resources: Next steps:		
	Lesson outline: Resources: Next steps:		
	Lesson outline: Resources: Next steps:		

Date/time/lesson	Subject(s):		Charge	Invoice info
	Lesson outline:			
	Resources:			
	Next steps:			
	Lesson outline:			
	Resources:			
	Next steps:			
	Lesson outline:			
	Resources:			
	Next steps:			
	Lesson outline:			
	Resources:			
	Next steps:			

Student name:
Email:

Location:
Phone:

Agency:
Word-of-mouth ☐   Website ☐
Facebook page ☐   Ads ☐

Additional needs:

Targets:
- _____ ☐   • _____ ☐
- _____ ☐   • _____ ☐
- _____   ☐

Date/time/ lesson	Subject(s):	Charge	Invoice info
	Lesson outline: Resources: Next steps:		
	Lesson outline: Resources: Next steps:		
	Lesson outline: Resources: Next steps:		

Date/time/ lesson	Subject(s):		Charge	Invoice info
	Lesson outline:			
	Resources:			
	Next steps:			
	Lesson outline:			
	Resources:			
	Next steps:			
	Lesson outline:			
	Resources:			
	Next steps:			
	Lesson outline:			
	Resources:			
	Next steps:			

Date/time/ lesson	Subject(s):	Charge	Invoice info
	Lesson outline: Resources: Next steps:		
	Lesson outline: Resources: Next steps:		
	Lesson outline: Resources: Next steps:		
	Lesson outline: Resources: Next steps:		

Date/time/lesson	Subject(s):		Charge	Invoice info
	Lesson outline:			
	Resources:			
	Next steps:			
	Lesson outline:			
	Resources:			
	Next steps:			
	Lesson outline:			
	Resources:			
	Next steps:			
	Lesson outline:			
	Resources:			
	Next steps:			

Student name:
Email:

Location:
Phone:

Agency:
Word-of-mouth ☐   Website ☐
Facebook page ☐   Ads ☐

Additional needs:

Targets:
- _____ ☐
- _____ ☐
- _____ ☐
- _____ ☐
- _____ ☐

Date/time/ lesson	Subject(s):	Charge	Invoice info
	Lesson outline: Resources: Next steps:		
	Lesson outline: Resources: Next steps:		
	Lesson outline: Resources: Next steps:		

Date/time/lesson	Subject(s):		Charge	Invoice info
	Lesson outline:			
	Resources:			
	Next steps:			
	Lesson outline:			
	Resources:			
	Next steps:			
	Lesson outline:			
	Resources:			
	Next steps:			
	Lesson outline:			
	Resources:			
	Next steps:			

Date/time/ lesson	Subject(s):	Charge	Invoice info
	Lesson outline: Resources: Next steps:		
	Lesson outline: Resources: Next steps:		
	Lesson outline: Resources: Next steps:		
	Lesson outline: Resources: Next steps:		

Date/time/lesson	Subject(s):	Charge	Invoice info
	Lesson outline: Resources: Next steps:		
	Lesson outline: Resources: Next steps:		
	Lesson outline: Resources: Next steps:		
	Lesson outline: Resources: Next steps:		

Student name:
Email:

Location:
Phone:

Agency:
Word-of-mouth ☐   Website ☐
Facebook page ☐   Ads ☐

Additional needs:

Targets:
- _____ ☐
- _____ ☐
- _____ ☐
- _____ ☐
- _____ ☐

Date/time/ lesson	Subject(s):	Charge	Invoice info
	Lesson outline: Resources:		
	Next steps:		
	Lesson outline: Resources:		
	Next steps:		
	Lesson outline: Resources:		
	Next steps:		

Date/time/ lesson	Subject(s):	Charge	Invoice info
	Lesson outline: Resources: Next steps:		
	Lesson outline: Resources: Next steps:		
	Lesson outline: Resources: Next steps:		
	Lesson outline: Resources: Next steps:		

Date/time/lesson	Subject(s):		Charge	Invoice info
	Lesson outline:			
	Resources:			
	Next steps:			
	Lesson outline:			
	Resources:			
	Next steps:			
	Lesson outline:			
	Resources:			
	Next steps:			
	Lesson outline:			
	Resources:			
	Next steps:			

Date/time/ lesson	Subject(s):	Charge	Invoice info
	Lesson outline: Resources: Next steps:		
	Lesson outline: Resources: Next steps:		
	Lesson outline: Resources: Next steps:		
	Lesson outline: Resources: Next steps:		

Student name:
Email:

Location:
Phone:

Agency:
Word-of-mouth ☐   Website ☐
Facebook page ☐   Ads ☐

Additional needs:

Targets:
- _____ ☐
- _____ ☐
- _____ ☐
- _____ ☐
- _____ ☐

Date/time/ lesson	Subject(s):	Charge	Invoice info
	Lesson outline: Resources: Next steps:		
	Lesson outline: Resources: Next steps:		
	Lesson outline: Resources: Next steps:		

Date/time/lesson	Subject(s):		Charge	Invoice info
	Lesson outline:			
	Resources:			
	Next steps:			
	Lesson outline:			
	Resources:			
	Next steps:			
	Lesson outline:			
	Resources:			
	Next steps:			
	Lesson outline:			
	Resources:			
	Next steps:			

Date/time/ lesson	Subject(s):		Charge	Invoice info
	Lesson outline:			
	Resources:			
	Next steps:			
	Lesson outline:			
	Resources:			
	Next steps:			
	Lesson outline:			
	Resources:			
	Next steps:			
	Lesson outline:			
	Resources:			
	Next steps:			

Date/time/lesson	Subject(s):		Charge	Invoice info
	Lesson outline:			
	Resources:			
	Next steps:			
	Lesson outline:			
	Resources:			
	Next steps:			
	Lesson outline:			
	Resources:			
	Next steps:			
	Lesson outline:			
	Resources:			
	Next steps:			

Student name:
Email:

Location:
Phone:

Agency:
Word-of-mouth ☐   Website ☐
Facebook page ☐   Ads ☐

Additional needs:

Targets:
- _____ ☐
- _____ ☐
- _____
- _____ ☐
- _____ ☐
  ☐

Date/time/ lesson	Subject(s):	Charge	Invoice info
	Lesson outline: Resources: Next steps:		
	Lesson outline: Resources: Next steps:		
	Lesson outline: Resources: Next steps:		

97

Date/time/ lesson	Subject(s):		Charge	Invoice info
	Lesson outline:			
	Resources:			
	Next steps:			
	Lesson outline:			
	Resources:			
	Next steps:			
	Lesson outline:			
	Resources:			
	Next steps:			
	Lesson outline:			
	Resources:			
	Next steps:			

Date/time/lesson	Subject(s):	Charge	Invoice info
	Lesson outline: Resources: Next steps:		
	Lesson outline: Resources: Next steps:		
	Lesson outline: Resources: Next steps:		
	Lesson outline: Resources: Next steps:		

Date/time/lesson	Subject(s):		Charge	Invoice info
	Lesson outline:			
	Resources:			
	Next steps:			
	Lesson outline:			
	Resources:			
	Next steps:			
	Lesson outline:			
	Resources:			
	Next steps:			
	Lesson outline:			
	Resources:			
	Next steps:			

Student name:
Email:

Location:
Phone:

Agency:
Word-of-mouth ☐   Website ☐
Facebook page ☐   Ads ☐

Additional needs:

Targets:
- _____ ☐
- _____ ☐
- _____ ☐
- _____ ☐
- _____ ☐

Date/time/lesson	Subject(s):	Charge	Invoice info
	Lesson outline: Resources: Next steps:		
	Lesson outline: Resources: Next steps:		
	Lesson outline: Resources: Next steps:		

Date/time/ lesson	Subject(s):		Charge	Invoice info
	Lesson outline:			
	Resources:			
	Next steps:			
	Lesson outline:			
	Resources:			
	Next steps:			
	Lesson outline:			
	Resources:			
	Next steps:			
	Lesson outline:			
	Resources:			
	Next steps:			

Date/time/lesson	Subject(s):	Charge	Invoice info
	Lesson outline: Resources: Next steps:		
	Lesson outline: Resources: Next steps:		
	Lesson outline: Resources: Next steps:		
	Lesson outline: Resources: Next steps:		

Date/time/lesson	Subject(s):	Charge	Invoice info
	Lesson outline: Resources: Next steps:		
	Lesson outline: Resources: Next steps:		
	Lesson outline: Resources: Next steps:		
	Lesson outline: Resources: Next steps:		

Printed in Great Britain
by Amazon